Costa B:

Travel Guide

2024

Discover the Charms, Culture, and Culinary Delights of Spain's Coastal Gem

Emily Catlett

EMILY CATLETT

EMILY CATLETT

MAP OF COSTA BRAVA

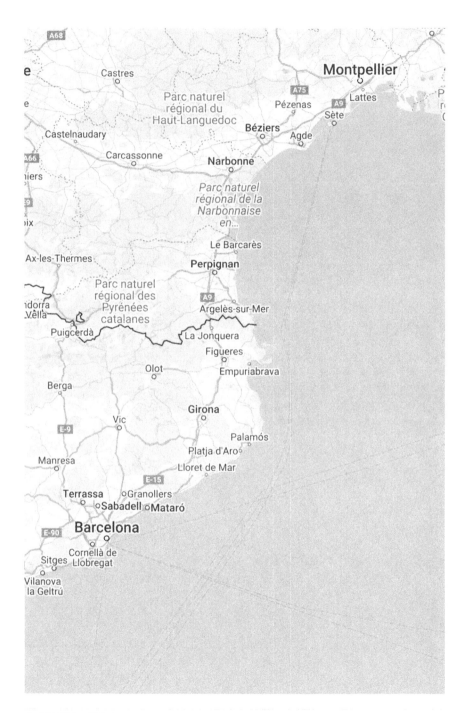

EMILY CATLETT

5 COSTA BRAVA TRAVEL GUIDE 2024

EMILY CATLETT

EMILY CATLETT

TABLE OF CONTENTS

7 COSTA BRAVA TRAVEL GUIDE 2024

EMILY CATLETT

10 COSTA BRAVA TRAVEL GUIDE 2024

I. INTRODUCTION TO COSTA BRAVA

In the heart of Catalonia, where the rocky mountains of the Pyrenees meet the brilliant blue seas of the Mediterranean, is a secret jewel that has caught my heart and mind. Costa Brava, a seaside paradise spanning along the northeastern coastlines of Spain, is a location of remarkable beauty and limitless surprises.

As a passionate traveler and storyteller, I've traveled through lovely towns, climbed along stunning coastal paths, eaten exquisite food, and immersed myself in the rich culture of Costa Brava. Each journey took me closer to the essence of this fascinating place, and I couldn't resist the impulse to share my enthusiasm and expertise with other wanderers seeking their own experiences.

In the pages of this handbook, I encourage you to go on an adventure like no other. Whether you're a seasoned adventurer or a first-time tourist, Costa Brava calls with its various landscapes, vivid history, and warm, inviting inhabitants. Allow me to be your company as we unearth secret coves, wander through ancient villages, and experience the flavors of Catalonia.

From the busy districts of Girona to the peaceful beaches of Calella de Palafrugell, every part of Costa Brava offers a distinct narrative waiting to be uncovered. With this handbook in hand, you'll travel this seaside paradise with confidence, acquiring insights and insider secrets that will convert your vacation into a memorable trip.

So, whether you're craving for a sun-soaked retreat, an investigation of ancient history, or just a taste of the Mediterranean's best, join me as we begin a tour around the enchanting Costa Brava. Together, we'll discover the mysteries, appreciate the beauty, and create memories that will last a lifetime. Welcome to my world of travel, where every page is a fresh beginning, and every chapter is an invitation to experience the unusual.

A. LOCATION AND GEOGRAPHY

1. Coastal Splendor:

Costa Brava, translated as "Wild Coast," spans along the Mediterranean Sea, encompassing around 214 kilometers (133 miles) of magnificent shoreline. The region's coastline landscape is distinguished by a steep, rocky terrain interlaced with peaceful coves and gorgeous beaches. The turquoise seas of the Mediterranean softly lap at its borders, providing a captivating contrast of land and sea.

2. Varied Landscapes:

The geography of Costa Brava is defined by its various landscapes. To the north, you'll discover the high peaks of the Pyrenees Mountains, which create a striking background to the seaside panorama. These mountains give good chances for trekking and adventure, affording spectacular views of the surrounding surroundings.

3. Charming Villages:

One of the beauties of Costa Brava is its picturesque beach communities, each with its character. From the colorful buildings of Cadaqués to the ancient lanes of Tossa de Mar, these communities are strewn along the coastline, snuggled against the background of green hills and cliffs. Their position makes them great for exploring and learning the true Spanish way of life.

4. Emporda Plains:

Inland from the shore, the Emporda Plains sprawl over the terrain. These lush lowlands are a significant element of Costa Brava's geography, sustaining agriculture and wineries. The vineyards produce some of Spain's best wines, giving a pleasant depth to the region's gastronomic offerings.

5. Unique Climate:

Costa Brava features a Mediterranean climate, characterized by mild winters and balmy summers. This environment makes it an excellent year-round vacation, as tourists may bask in the Mediterranean sun during the summer months or discover the region's beauty in the colder seasons without the high temperatures experienced in other regions of Spain.

6. Breathtaking Natural Reserves:

The locale of Costa Brava is also home to various natural reserves and parks, including the Cap de Creus Natural Park and the Aiguamolls de l'Empordà Natural Park. These protected areas reflect the region's tremendous biodiversity, with various flora and wildlife that flourish in the distinctive Mediterranean ecology.

7. Coastal Pathways:

For nature aficionados and adventure seekers, Costa Brava provides the GR 92 coastal footpath, a network of hiking paths that weave their way down the coast. This enables you to explore the geography of the area up close, allowing possibilities to find secret coves, rocky cliffs, and magnificent vistas.

B. HISTORY AND CULTURE

The region's name, Costa Brava, translates to "Wild Coast," an appropriate nickname for a place that has craggy cliffs, crystal-clear seas, and secret coves waiting to be found. Its visual splendor alone is enough to inspire awe and astonishment, but it is the area's rich and varied history that sets it unique.

Dating back as early as the Paleolithic period, the area has been inhabited by many tribes, each leaving their stamp on the terrain. From the Celts and Iberians to the Romans and Moors, the Costa Brava has been molded by a variety of civilizations, resulting in a melting pot of history and legacy.

One of the most famous and significant civilizations in the region's history was the Roman Empire. The Romans came in the 3rd century BC and reigned over the province until the 5th century AD. They left their legacy in the shape of stunning architectural wonders, such as the huge remains of Empúries, a city built by the Greeks but subsequently taken over and extended by the Romans. These historic remains serve as a tribute to the grandeur and influence of the Roman Empire and give significant insights into the everyday lives of its citizens.

Following the collapse of the Romans, the Moors came in the 8th century and swiftly captured significant portions of the Iberian Peninsula, including the Costa Brava. The Moors were famed for their outstanding architectural and agricultural talents, which may still be seen today in the region's typical whitewashed houses and terraced terrain. Despite their short-lived control, the Moors left a lasting effect on the culture of the Costa Brava.

In succeeding years, the area became a battlefield between the Christian kingdoms and the Muslim monarchs during the Reconquista. The medieval fortifications and castles that dot the shoreline are a tribute to this turbulent epoch in the area's history. These old monuments, such as the Castell de Begur and the Castle of Tossa de Mar, serve as a reminder of the trials and achievements of the people who struggled for dominance over the Costa Brava.

Today, the Costa Brava is a dynamic combination of old-world beauty and contemporary influences. Its coastal cities and villages are a blend of many cultures, expressed in the local food, customs, and festivals. Each town has its particular character, from the busy city of Girona with its well-preserved medieval district to the charming fishing hamlet of Cadaqués, widely known as the birthplace of surrealist artist Salvador Dalí.

The Costa Brava's cultural heritage is also on full show during its various festivals and festivities. From the blazing Correfoc (fire run) at the Festa Major de Gràcia in Barcelona to the colorful Castellers (human towers) in Tarragona, these events bring people together to celebrate the region's unique history.

C. WHY VISIT IN 2024?

One of the primary reasons to visit Costa Brava in 2024 is its gorgeous beaches. With over 200 kilometers of coastline, this area has some of the most magnificent beaches in Europe. From hidden coves to extensive lengths of golden sand, there is a beach for every style of tourist. Breath-taking blue seas and stunning scenery provide for a postcard-worthy location, great for resting and unwinding. Whether you want to soak up the sun, try out water sports, or just enjoy a leisurely walk down the sand, the beaches of Costa Brava offer everything.

Apart from its magnificent beaches, Costa Brava is home to other quaint coastal villages that are worth seeing. Each town has its particular character and charm, allowing a look into the region's rich history and culture. For a sense of true Spanish living, visit places like Tossa de Mar, Begur, and Cadaqués. These small villages are excellent for roaming about, enjoying the classic architecture, and eating some wonderful local food. In 2024, these communities will also be organizing numerous cultural festivals and events, providing visitors the opportunity to explore the local traditions and customs.

If you are a fan of the great outdoors, Costa Brava will not disappoint. With its different landscapes, this area provides a selection of activities for nature aficionados. From trekking in the cliffs of Cap de Creus Natural Park to discovering the volcanic landscapes of La Garrotxa, there is something for everyone. In addition to its natural beauty, Costa Brava is also home to various historic monuments, like the medieval town of Besalú and the ruins of Empúries, allowing an insight into the region's history.

Moreover, 2024 celebrates the 50th anniversary of the Costa Brava and Pyrenees of Girona brand, providing another motivation to visit this gorgeous area. This milestone will be marked with unique events and activities throughout the year, giving it the ideal opportunity to immerse yourself in the region's rich culture, customs, and festivities.

Last but not least, Costa Brava is a foodie's heaven. With its seaside setting, fresh seafood is a must-try, along with other traditional meals like paella and fideuà. The area is also famed for its wine, with numerous vineyards producing great wines that are worth drinking. In 2024, the area will also be holding a Food and Wine Festival, exhibiting the finest of Costa Brava's gastronomic pleasures.

CHAPTER 1

II. PLANNING YOUR TRIP

A. BEST TIME TO VISIT

The main tourist season in Costa Brava spans from June to September, when the weather is bright and sunny, making it suitable for beach activities and water sports. However, the months of July and August have the biggest flood of visitors, causing the rates of rooms and activities to surge. If you want a calmer and more budget-friendly experience, it's advisable to avoid these months.

For those who wish to avoid the crowds and experience Costa Brava's beauty in its most calm condition, the shoulder seasons of April to May and September to October are the perfect times to come. During these months, the weather is still nice, and the water is warm enough for swimming. Not to mention, the blossoming spring flowers and autumn leaves add to the appeal of the location. Moreover, you'll have a greater selection of alternatives for hotels, and you'll also be able to catch some amazing prices.

If you're a lover of outdoor activities like hiking, riding, and exploring nature, then the ideal time to visit Costa Brava would be during the low season from November to March. While the temperatures may be on the colder side, the weather is typically warm and nice for outdoor excursions. Plus, you'll have the added pleasure of enjoying the region's famed events, such as the Carnival of Roses and the Girona Flower Festival.

One thing to note while planning your vacation to Costa Brava is that the area has a Mediterranean climate. This implies that you may anticipate warm temperatures and sunny days throughout the year. However, it's always a good idea to check the weather prediction before your trip, since unexpected rain showers and cold winds may occur even during the peak tourist season.

B. VISA REQUIREMENTS

As a member of the European Union, people of other EU nations do not require a visa to access Costa Brava. They may just utilize their legitimate national ID or passport for entrance. However, for non-EU nationals, a visa is necessary to enter Costa Brava. It is crucial to examine the exact rules for your place of origin before organizing your trip.

The two kinds of visas that enable admission into Costa Brava are the Schengen visa and the Spanish visa. The Schengen visa is valid for 26 countries in Europe, including Spain, and allows for repeated entry for 90 days. The Spanish visa is intended for people wishing to visit solely Spain and is valid for a longer term of stay.

To get a Schengen visa, you will need to apply at the Spanish embassy or consulate in your place of residency. The application procedure normally entails filling out a form, giving a valid passport, passport-sized pictures, a travel itinerary, and evidence of adequate finances to cover your stay in Costa Brava.

Furthermore, you will need to produce evidence of travel insurance that covers medical expenditures up to €30,000 and includes repatriation charges. It is also essential to obtain travel insurance that covers trip cancellation or interruption coverage.

The embassy or consulate may also request extra documentation, depending on your unique circumstances. This might include evidence of lodging, round-way airplane tickets, proof of job or study, and a cover letter outlining the purpose of your trip.

It is crucial to know that the visa application procedure might take up to several weeks, so it is advisable to prepare and apply in advance. The cost of a Schengen visa is presently €80, and it is non-refundable, even if your application is refused.

If you want to remain in Costa Brava for the long term, it is vital to comply with the visa restrictions to prevent any complications with immigration officials. Overstaying your visa may result in penalties, deportation, and a restriction on future trips.

C. CURRENCY AND LANGUAGE

Firstly, let's discuss about money. Costa Brava, like the rest of Spain, utilizes the Euro as its official currency. This implies that tourists from countries that do not use the Euro will need to convert their cash before or upon arrival. Fortunately, there are lots of currency exchange offices and ATMs accessible across the area, making it easier for tourists to get local money. It is crucial to remember that credit and debit cards are commonly accepted at most businesses, but it is always wise to carry some cash for minor purchases and transactions.

Another issue to bear in mind when it comes to money is budgeting. It is crucial to get an approximate concept of how much money you will need throughout your stay in Costa Brava. This may help you plan your spending and ensure that you have enough to cover your hotel, meals, transportation, and any other activities or mementos you may like to buy.

Now, let's move on to language. The official language of Costa Brava, as well as the rest of Spain, is Spanish. However, owing to its prominence as a tourist destination, many inhabitants also speak English, especially in large towns and tourism regions. This makes it quite straightforward for English-speaking guests to converse and find their way about the area.

However, for those wishing to truly immerse themselves in the local culture and travel off the main route, understanding some basic Spanish words may go a long way. Not only will it make interactions with locals easier, but it also displays a degree of respect for the nation and its people.

Furthermore, knowing a few important words in the local language may enrich your whole travel experience, from ordering a meal at a local restaurant to bartering at a market. It provides for a stronger connection with the nation and its people, making your journey more meaningful and unforgettable.

D. ACCOMMODATIONS OPTIONS

HOTELS:

1. Hotel Alàbriga - S'Agaró

Elevating luxury to new heights, Hotel Alàbriga is more than simply a place to stay; it's an experience in itself. This hotel blends contemporary elegance with comfort, providing rooms that enjoy beautiful views of the Mediterranean. The in-house restaurant, managed by a famous chef, dishes up gastronomic delicacies that are a feast for both the eyes and the taste. The hotel also boasts a state-of-the-art spa, great for resting after a day of visiting the Costa Brava.

2. Hostal de La Gavina - S'Agaró

A combination of historic beauty and contemporary conveniences, Hostal de La Gavina is a jewel on the Costa Brava. Situated close to the sea, this hotel provides accommodations with outstanding views and décor that radiate old-world elegance. The highlight is their wonderfully kept grounds and the outdoor pool, which appears right out of a fairy tale. Their fine dining alternatives are a treat, presenting local Catalan food with a flair.

3. Hotel Aigua Blava - Begur

Overlooking the lovely bays of Fornells and Aiguablava, Hotel Aigua Blava provides a tranquil respite. The hotel's rooms and villas are large, with a hint of Mediterranean style, affording spectacular sea views. You may enjoy a choice of sports, including diving and sailing, or relax on the local beaches. The hotel's restaurant is recognized for its traditional Catalan specialties, which are a must-try for culinary connoisseurs.

4. Spa & Hotel Mas de Torrent - Torrent

This property is the ultimate of rustic luxury. Set in a renovated 18th-century Catalan farmhouse, Mas de Torrent is surrounded by beautiful gardens and provides an intimate and serene setting. The rooms are built with a combination of modern and rustic features, providing a warm ambiance. The spa, with its choice of treatments, is a refuge for relaxation. The hotel's restaurant, with its locally produced ingredients and traditional Catalan dishes, gives an authentic sense of the area.

5. Hotel Cala del Pi - Platja d'Aro

This luxury hotel is perched on the brink of a cliff, affording panoramic views of the Mediterranean. Hotel Cala del Pi mixes refinement with comfort. The apartments are tastefully equipped, many with their patios overlooking the sea. The highlight is their direct access to a secluded beach, delivering a private piece of heaven. The spa is fantastic, and the dining experience is top-notch, with an emphasis on seafood and local products.

VILLAS:

1. Villa Maravilla:

Overlooking the peaceful seas of the Mediterranean, Villa Maravilla is a gem of modern design and comfort. This property features enormous living rooms that effortlessly blend with outside terraces, affording stunning views of the sea. The infinity pool seems to blend with the ocean, providing a sensation of endless splendor. Each bedroom is a sanctuary of quiet, with big windows that welcome the early light. The villa's contemporary kitchen is outfitted with high-end gadgets, making it a delight for people who love to cook.

2. Casa Tranquila:

Set in the center of a verdant garden, Casa Tranquila is a hideaway for people seeking a calm escape. This classic Spanish property mixes rustic beauty with contemporary facilities, giving a warm and welcoming setting. The outside area contains a gorgeous pool surrounded by aromatic flowers and natural plants, providing a secluded paradise. Inside, the property is furnished with local art and handmade furnishings, contributing to its particular character. The warm living area and well-appointed bedrooms guarantee a comfortable stay for families or parties.

3. El Refugio de la Costa:

This architecturally magnificent property is a genuine jewel, blending luxury with environmental sustainability. El Refugio de la Costa is created with eco-friendly materials and has solar panels, making it suitable for eco-conscious guests. The interior is a combination of simplicity and elegance, with open areas that are both utilitarian and elegant. The centerpiece is the outside area, boasting a saltwater pool and a huge terrace for al fresco eating, all set against the background of the rolling hills of Costa Brava.

4. La Casa de los Sueños:

Offering an outstanding perspective of the craggy coastline, La Casa de los Sueños is a magnificent getaway for people who love the finest things in life. This villa's design emphasizes comfort and elegance, with luxurious furniture and state-of-the-art conveniences. The outside space contains a heated pool, a Jacuzzi, and a grill area, excellent for entertaining. The bedrooms are intended for comfort, with soft lighting and luxury linen, assuring a good night's sleep.

5. Villa Alegria:

Located only steps away from a quiet beach, Villa Alegria is the ideal combination of beachfront serenity and grandeur. This home has immediate access to the sandy shoreline, making it perfect for beach enthusiasts. The interior is light and open, with huge windows that let in the sea breeze. The open-plan living area is great for social events, while the individual balconies adjacent to each bedroom give a peaceful spot to watch the sunset.

APARTMENTS:

1. Seaview Splendor, Lloret de Mar

Overlooking the blue seas of Lloret de Mar, Seaview Splendor is a dream come true for sea lovers. This contemporary property includes floor-to-ceiling windows, enabling you to wake up to stunning beach views every day. The big terrace is great for enjoying your morning coffee or an evening drink of local wine. Inside, the apartment is decorated with a modern flare, offering comfort without sacrificing elegance. The two-bedroom configuration makes it suitable for families or small groups.

2. Garden Oasis, Calella de Palafrugell

Tucked away in the lovely village of Calella de Palafrugell, Garden Oasis is a tranquil getaway. This ground-floor apartment opens out to a lovely private garden, where you can rest beneath the shade of olive trees. The room is attractively designed, with local art and typical Spanish elements. With two nice bedrooms and a fully equipped kitchen, it's an ideal home away from home. The condo is only a short walk from some of the region's top beaches and eating locations.

3. Historic Haven, Girona

For people who appreciate history and architecture, Historic Haven in Girona is a must-stay. Located in the center of the old town, this apartment is set in a wonderfully restored structure. The mix of historic stone walls with contemporary utilities produces a distinctive and pleasant living place. The balcony gives beautiful views of the ancient city, especially the famed Girona Cathedral. It's a one-bedroom apartment, suitable for couples or lone visitors seeking a combination of history and comfort.

4. Beachfront Bliss, Roses

Situated directly on the sands of Roses, Beachfront Bliss provides an unparalleled position. This contemporary apartment features a sleek design with all the latest comforts you could wish for. The highlight is the immediate beach access — simply step outside, and you're on the sandy sands of one of Costa Brava's most gorgeous beaches. The apartment includes three bedrooms, making it a wonderful alternative for big families or groups of friends.

5. Mountain View Retreat, Begur

Located amid the slopes of Begur, Mountain View Retreat is a retreat for people seeking solitude. The property provides wonderful views of the neighboring mountains and farmland. The interior is warm and pleasant, with a fireplace adding to its attractiveness. It's wonderful for those chilly nights when you want to curl up with a book. With two bedrooms and a wide living space, it's excellent for families or small parties. The vibrant town heart of Begur is only a short drive away, providing fantastic eating and shopping.

CAMPSITES:

1. El Delfín Verde - Torroella de Montgrí

El Delfín Verde, nestled in the middle of the Bay of Roses, is a paradise for beach lovers and families. This wide campground provides direct access to a superb sandy beach, giving a great combination of leisure and pleasure. It's not just about sunbathing; the complex has a big swimming pool shaped like a dolphin, entertaining entertainment for youngsters, and a range of sports facilities. The campground also gives a rare chance to visit the surrounding Montgrí Natural Park, a jewel for nature aficionados.

2. Tossa de Mar's Cala Llevadó Camping

For those wanting a more quiet and natural location, Camping Cala Llevadó is a good option. Situated in the ancient town of Tossa de Mar, this campground is famed for its lovely terraced plots that give spectacular views of the four nearby beaches. Hikers will adore the paths that weave through the surrounding woodlands, leading to secret coves and spectacular overlooks. The campsite's dedication to sustainability and maintaining the natural beauty of its surroundings makes it a responsible option for eco-conscious guests.

3. Camping Sant Pere Pescador - La Ballena Alegre

This bustling campground, situated close to the beach, is a hotspot for windsurfers and kite surfers thanks to the outstanding wind conditions of the Gulf of Roses. Camping La Ballena Alegre is not only about water activities; it's a full-fledged resort featuring beautiful bungalows, a health center, and several eating choices. The campground provides an assortment of activities for all ages, ensuring that every member of the family has a great visit.

4. Camping Treumal - Calonge

Overlooking the Bay of Palamós, Camping Treumal is a calm escape. Its immediate access to a tranquil private beach makes it perfect for anyone wishing to escape the noise and bustle. The campground is recognized for its beautiful, well-maintained grounds and its typical Mediterranean architecture, which delivers an authentic Spanish camping experience. The surrounding fishing hamlet of Palamós, noted for its delicious seafood, is a must-visit for gourmet connoisseurs.

5. Camping Cypsela Resort - Pals

Located adjacent to the historic town of Pals, Camping Cypsela Resort is a high-end camping resort. This five-star campground is great for people who want a touch of luxury in their camping experience. It boasts a top-notch pool complex, sports facilities, and high-quality housing alternatives. Its closeness to some of the greatest golf courses in the area makes it a favorite among golfing fans. The campground also gives convenient access to the stunning beaches of Costa Brava and the ancient monuments of Pals.

EMILY CATLETT

CHAPTER 2

III. MUST-SEE DESTINATIONS

A. COASTAL TOWNS

1. CADAQUÉS

As you travel around Cadaqués, the first thing that hits you is the magnificent contrast of the dazzling white houses against the deep blue of the Mediterranean Sea. This lovely village was once a favorite hideaway for the great surrealist artist Salvador Dalí, and it's easy to understand how the stunning scenery might inspire such creativity. The Salvador Dalí House-Museum in Portlligat, a little community just outside Cadaqués, is a must-visit for art fans. It's not simply a museum; it's a voyage inside the mind of a genius, with unique designs and bizarre installations.

Cadaqués isn't simply about its artistic past. The town is a paradise for cuisine enthusiasts also. Seafood, fresh from the Mediterranean, is a mainstay here. Imagine having a dinner of freshly caught fish, seasoned with local herbs, while you sit in a quaint coastal restaurant. The tastes are as real as they get, encapsulating the spirit of Catalan cuisine.

For those who enjoy the outdoors, the surrounding region of Cadaqués provides many of chances. The Cap de Creus Natural Park, with its cliffs and isolated bays, is a delight for hikers and nature enthusiasts. The views from the cliffs are stunning, presenting a panorama of the sea and the rough coastline. It's a fantastic position to see the sunset, as the sky changes into a painting of oranges and pinks.

Cadaqués also has a strong cultural calendar. Throughout the year, the town holds many festivals and events that exhibit local customs and arts. From music festivals to traditional Catalan holidays, these events give a glimpse into the dynamic community spirit of Cadaqués.

2. TOSSA DE MAR

1. Getting There

Tossa de Mar is conveniently accessible from major towns in Spain and Europe. The closest airport is Girona-Costa Brava, situated about 40 minutes away, with direct flights from major European cities including London, Berlin, and Paris. You may also reach the town by rail or bus from Barcelona, which takes roughly 1.5 hours. Whichever method of transportation you pick, the gorgeous ride will be worth the reward.

2. Historic Landmarks

One cannot speak about Tossa de Mar without mentioning its most famous sight, the Vila Vella, a walled medieval village built on a hill near the sea. It is regarded as one of the best-preserved walled towns on the Mediterranean coast, with narrow cobblestone lanes and classic whitewashed buildings. Take a stroll around the walls and see spectacular views of the sea and surrounding area. Don't miss the Chapel of Our Lady of Socorro, one of the town's most photographed landmarks.

3. Beaches

Tossa de Mar is home to some of the most stunning beaches in Spain. The biggest and most popular one is the Platja Gran, a crescent-shaped beach with crystal blue waves, golden sand, and a background of picturesque rocks. For a more private experience, travel to the Platja d'es Codolar, famed for its quiet ambiance and magnificent stone formations. If you're feeling brave, take a boat journey to the neighboring secret coves and explore more of Tossa de Mar's natural splendor.

4. Cultural Activities

Apart from its natural and historical features, Tossa de Mar also provides a range of cultural events. Visit the Municipal Museum to learn about the town's heritage and its links to notable painters like Marc Chagall and André Masson, who lived and worked here. For art connoisseurs, the Museum of Contemporary Art shows works by local and international artists. Don't miss the vibrant weekly market, where you may discover local products, crafts, and souvenirs.

5. Local Cuisine

Indulge in the tastes of authentic Catalan cuisine at Tossa de Mar's various restaurants and pubs. Try the famed paella, a delicious rice meal with a variety of seafood and meats, or experience some of the local delicacies, such as "suquet de peix", a robust seafood stew. For a delicious treat, don't miss out on the "crema catalana", a creamy custard dish covered with caramelized sugar.

6. Accommodations

Tossa de Mar provides a selection of lodgings to suit every budget. From opulent beach resorts to charming boutique hotels, there is something for everyone. For those wanting a more genuine experience, stay in one of the town's beautiful bed & breakfasts, many of which are situated in old houses.

3. BEGUR

Getting to Begur Costa Brava is straightforward, with various transit alternatives available. The nearest airport is Girona Airport, which is slightly under an hour's drive away. From there, you may hire a vehicle or take a bus to reach Begur. Alternatively, you may go by rail to the adjacent cities of Girona or Figueres and then take a bus or cab to Begur.

Upon entering, you will be instantly attracted by the wonderful atmosphere of Begur Costa Brava. Its ancient lanes flanked with old stone homes and quaint fishermen's huts form a lovely environment that will take you back in time. Take a walk and observe the whitewashed buildings covered with bright bougainvillea and the small passageways that lead to hidden squares and secret gardens.

One of the must-see sites in Begur is the renowned Castle of Begur, built on a mountaintop above the settlement. This 11th-century castle gives stunning views of the surrounding coastline, and its well-preserved remains are a tribute to the rich history of this area. You may also explore the neighboring remnants of Begur's ancient defensive walls, which are a reminder of the village's status as a defensive bastion.

For beach enthusiasts, Begur Costa Brava features some of the most magnificent and quiet beaches in Spain. The crystal-clear seas and secret coves are great for swimming, snorkeling, or just resting with a book and soaking up the sun. Sa Riera, Aigua Blava, and Tamariu are some of the most popular beaches in the region, but for a calmer experience, travel to the lesser-known beaches of Sa Tuna and Fornells.

Furthermore, to its natural beauty, Begur is also recognized for its superb local food. The hamlet features a blend of traditional Catalan foods and contemporary fusion cuisine, making it a food lover's heaven. Don't miss eating the famed seafood dishes, including paella, fideuà, and suquet de peix (fish stew).

For a unique and genuine experience, try staying in one of Begur's numerous beautiful boutique hotels or guesthouses. These hotels are generally situated in historic buildings and provide customized service and a comfortable setting. If you want a little more luxury, you may choose one of the beautiful villas or resorts with amazing views of the sea.

Begur Costa Brava is also an ideal location for touring the nearby towns and villages. Renting a vehicle and enjoying a picturesque drive down the coastline can bring you to other attractive coastal villages, such as Calella de Palafrugell, Llafranc, and Palamós. You may also take a day excursion to the adjacent city of Girona, noted for its well-preserved medieval old town and famous for being a shooting site for the blockbuster TV series, "Game of Thrones."

EMILY CATLETT

B. NATURAL ATTRACTIONS

1. CAP DE CREUS NATIONAL PARK

Getting to Cap de Creus National Park is straightforward, with Girona-Costa Brava Airport approximately a 1-hour drive away. From there, you may hire a vehicle or take a bus to reach the park. The magnificent journey down the coast will instantly set the tone for your vacation, with spectacular cliffs and panoramic views of the Mediterranean Sea. As you approach the park, you will be welcomed by a diversified environment of rugged mountains, rolling hills, and meandering paths that lead to secret coves and isolated beaches.

One of the attractions of visiting Cap de Creus National Park is exploring its various hiking routes. With over 24 defined pathways to select from, you may immerse yourself in the park's natural beauties at your speed. For a more strenuous trip, trek up to the highest mountain, Puig de Les Salines, where you will be rewarded with stunning views of the surrounding area. Along the trip, you will discover a variety of plant and animal species, including the rare Mediterranean tortoise and some of Europe's most stunning wildflowers.

If you want to explore the park by sea, you may hire a kayak and paddle along the crystal blue seas. As you float past secluded coves and little bays, you will be surrounded by stunning cliffs and rock formations. For a more leisurely boat journey, take a cruise to the tiny fishing hamlet of Cadaqués, one of the most picturesque places on the Costa Brava. Cadaqués is also home to the famed Salvador Dali Museum, which contains a collection of the renowned artist's works.

For a flavor of local culture, explore the little towns and villages sprinkled around the park. In the town of El Port de la Selva, you may indulge in real Catalan cuisine, including fresh fish and local specialties such as rice dishes and cured meats. You may also visit the picturesque alleys of Port Lligat, where Dali's old house and studio, now a museum, can be discovered.

As you wind down your journey in Cap de Creus National Park, be sure to take some time to relax and absorb in the calm surroundings. With no lack of gorgeous sites, you may locate the ideal spot to relax and watch the sunset over the Mediterranean Sea or have a picnic with a view.

2. GIRONA PYRENEES

From the rough mountains of the Pyrenees to the lovely Mediterranean shore, this area provides spectacular scenery at every turn. Immerse yourself in nature as you trek through lush green valleys, bathe in crystal-clear lakes, or ski in the snowy peaks. You may also go on a hot air balloon flight to obtain a bird's eye perspective of the magnificent countryside.

For those interested in history and culture, Girona Pyrenees Costa Brava boasts a plethora of ancient monuments, castles, and medieval villages ready to be explored. The city of Girona itself has a well-preserved Jewish Quarter, a Gothic cathedral, and old Roman fortifications. Take a walk through the lovely cobblestone streets and immerse yourself in the colorful ambiance of this busy city.

Indulge in the native food and sample the unique tastes of Catalonia. From fresh fish to substantial stews, the cuisine of Girona Pyrenees Costa Brava is a celebration of local products and age-old traditions. Don't miss the chance to try the great local wines, many of which are made directly in this area.

One of the features of Girona Pyrenees Costa Brava is its gorgeous coastline, known as the Costa Brava. With almost 200km of cliffs, gorgeous coves, and sandy beaches, it's heaven for beach lovers and water enthusiasts. You may enjoy a leisurely boat cruise around the coast, try scuba diving in the beautiful seas, or just rest on the golden dunes.

But Girona Pyrenees Costa Brava provides much more than simply natural beauty and cultural charm. It's also a fantastic place for adventure enthusiasts. With sports such as mountain biking, rock climbing, and paragliding, you'll be able to get your adrenaline racing in no time.

To make the most of your vacation, be sure to book a visit during one of the regions numerous festivals. From the traditional Castellera human towers to the bright Flower Festival, these events give a unique view into the local way of life and are guaranteed to make a lasting impression.

When it comes to lodgings, Girona Pyrenees Costa Brava boasts a range of alternatives to fit any traveler's requirements. From luxurious resorts to budget-friendly hostels, there's something for every budget. For a unique experience, try staying at one of the region's lovely agritourism sites, where you may stay on a working farm and experience authentic rural life.

3. AIGUAMOLLS DE L'EMPORDÀ

1. Location:

Located along the coast of northern Catalonia, Aiguamolls de l'Empordà is readily accessible from famous places such as Barcelona and Girona. It encompasses an area of almost 5,000 hectares and is separated into two major sections: the northern portion is known as the Aiguamolls Natural Park and the southern part is the Aiguamolls National Park.

2. Nature and Wildlife:

EMILY CATLETT

The Aiguamolls de l'Empordà is a delight for nature enthusiasts. Its gorgeous terrain is formed of sandy beaches, dunes, lagoons, and marshes. The reserve is home to hundreds of kinds of flora and animals, making it a wonderful site for bird-watching. Over 300 different kinds of birds have been observed here, including flamingos, herons, and storks.

3. Activities:

One of the finest ways to experience the reserve is by walking or cycling along the different routes. Along the trip, you'll experience a range of environments, from reed meadows to oak woods. Guided excursions are also provided for anyone who wishes to learn more about the reserve's biodiversity and history.

For a more adventurous experience, travelers may kayak through the canals and lagoons, viewing birds and other species along the way. The reserve also provides horseback riding and horse-drawn carriage trips for a unique view of the countryside.

4. Cultural and Historical sites:

Aiguamolls de l'Empordà also has a rich cultural and historical history. The reserve was formerly utilized for agriculture and fishing, which has sculpted the terrain and contributed to its diversified environment. There are also vestiges of old villages and archeological sites that may be investigated inside the reserve.

Nearby, there are delightful traditional towns with tiny cobblestone streets, where you can immerse yourself in the local culture and sample great regional food.

5. Best time to visit:

The greatest time to visit Aiguamolls de l'Empordà is between the spring and fall months when the weather is moderate and the reserve is alive with migrating birds. However, the reserve may be experienced all year round, since each season provides a distinct experience.

6. Practical Information:

Entrance at Aiguamolls de l'Empordà is free, however, tourists are requested to give a gift to assist the conservation efforts. The reserve is available all year round, however opening hours may change according to the season. There are well-maintained picnic spots inside the reserve, making it an excellent destination for a day excursion.

C. HISTORIC SITES

1. DALI THEATRE-MUSEUM

The edifice, built by Dali himself, is a piece of art in its own right. Its odd facade, covered with huge eggs and sculptures, hints at the bizarre sights that lie within. As you go inside the museum, you'll be welcomed by the renowned surrealist wall, containing a series of plaster casts of Dali's face, signifying the artist's preoccupation with self-representation.

As you make your way around the museum, you'll be treated to a voyage through Dali's life and paintings. From his first works to his last masterpieces, the museum's collection displays the progression of his distinctive style. It comprises paintings, sculptures, and installations that vary from the weird and dreamy to the thought-provoking and contentious.

One of the centerpieces of the museum is the Mae West chamber, a life-size installation inspired by the characteristics of the iconic American actress. As you approach the room, it seems as if you're going into a gigantic face, with a sofa positioned exactly to give the appearance of her lips. This masterwork is a tribute to Dali's passion for optical illusions and his ability to challenge the viewer's vision.

Another must-see is the Dome Room, a grandiose area covered with a spectacular glass dome and packed with an assortment of sculptures and paintings. The grandeur of this space is likely to leave you in awe and enable you to properly comprehend the magnitude and intricacy of Dali's art.

Apart from the art, the museum also offers a courtyard where visitors may rest and have a drink or a snack at the café. You may also peruse the enormous gift store, where you'll discover a broad choice of souvenirs and literature relating to Dali and his work.

When planning your visit to the Dali Theatre Museum, it's crucial to understand that it may become rather crowded, particularly during high tourist seasons. To completely immerse oneself in the exhibitions, aim to visit early in the morning or later in the day. You may also buy your tickets online in advance to escape the lineups and save time.

2. ROMAN RUINS IN EMPÚRIES

History of Empúries:

The town of Empúries was built by the Greeks in the 6th century BC, making it one of the oldest communities on the Costa Brava. However, it was the Romans who left the most marked stamp on the town during their conquest of the Iberian Peninsula in the 3rd century BC. The Roman city of Empúries was an important port for commerce and a significant center for agriculture, making it an affluent and prominent hub throughout the Roman period. However, the settlement subsequently decayed and was later abandoned owing to barbarian raids and natural calamities.

Top Roman Ruins to Visit:

1. The Forum: The center of each Roman city, the Forum at Empúries is a vast public area adorned with majestic columns. It was the social, political, and economic hub of the town, and today, tourists may roam about the remains and picture the hustle and bustle of ordinary Roman life.

2. The Basilica: This enormous edifice was once a temple devoted to the Capitoline Triad of gods: Jupiter, Juno, and Minerva. It subsequently became a law court under the Roman Empire. Today, tourists may still enjoy its majestic walls and columns, as well as a lovely mosaic floor representing marine animals.

3. The Roman Houses: These well-preserved residences provide a peek into the everyday life of the rich Roman people of Empúries. The mosaics and frescoes that cover the walls are a monument to the creative and ornamental inclinations of the period.

4. The Greek Port: Before the advent of the Romans, the Greeks erected a port at Empúries. Visitors may wander around the old docks and envision the busy commerce that took place here centuries ago.

Tips for Visiting:

1. Wear comfortable shoes: The ruins span a huge area, and you will be doing a lot of walking. Make sure you wear comfy shoes to thoroughly enjoy your stay.

2. Visit in the morning: The ruins may become busy in the afternoons, so it is recommended to visit in the morning to escape the crowds and the heat.

3. Guided tour: Consider taking a guided tour to understand more about the history and importance of the ruins. The advisors are incredibly informed and will improve your experience.

4. Visit the museum: Before or after exploring the ruins, be sure to stop by the Empúries Museum, which includes numerous relics and exhibitions relating to the Roman and Greek history of the town.

5. Take lots of water and sunscreen: The Costa Brava may be hot, and the ruins do not give much shade. Be prepared with drink and sunscreen to remain hydrated and protected from the sun.

3. MEDIEVAL VILLAGES

1. Tossa de Mar:

Located on the southern end of Costa Brava, Tossa de Mar is a lovely medieval town with a rich history reaching back to the 12th century. As you meander through its small winding lanes, you'll be taken back in time with its well-preserved historic walls, traditional dwellings, and cute little businesses. The centerpiece of this community is its majestic 12th-century castle, Vila Vella, set on top of a hill overlooking the sea. You may also visit the Municipal Museum situated in the ancient Governor's Palace to learn about the town's history.

2. Pals:

Pals is another medieval hamlet that will transport you back in time with its cobblestone alleys, old stone homes, and stunning Romanesque architecture. Walk around the well-preserved city walls and bask in the spectacular views of the surrounding landscape. Make sure to see the Torre de les Hores, a 15th-century watchtower that is now a museum depicting the town's history. Don't forget to enjoy some local specialties like the famed Catalan rice dish, paella, at one of the traditional eateries.

3. Peratallada:

Known as one of the most beautiful medieval towns in Spain, Peratallada is a must-visit for its well-preserved castle, historic walls, and typical buildings constructed of golden sandstone. Stroll around its lovely streets and appreciate the fine features of the buildings. Don't miss out on visiting the Sant Esteve church, which gives spectacular views of the hamlet from its bell tower. Peratallada is well recognized for its culinary scene, so please sample the local delights at one of the numerous restaurants.

4. Besalú:

Located in the Garrotxa area, Besalú is a lovely medieval town with a spectacular Romanesque bridge that joins the two sides of the settlement. As you cross the bridge, you'll be met with the stately 11th-century castle and the spectacular arches of the Plaça dels Jueus plaza. The town is also home to one of the finest preserved Jewish neighborhoods in Europe, which you may explore via its small streets and lanes.

5. Cadaqués:

No vacation to Costa Brava is complete without visiting Cadaqués, a lovely seaside town noted for its white-washed cottages, tiny alleyways, and breathtaking sea vistas. The town's most renowned citizen, Salvador Dali, has immortalized Cadaqués in many of his artworks. Take a walk along its scenic shoreline or visit the Dali House Museum, the artist's former apartment, to discover more about his life and work. Cadaqués is also famed for its delicious seafood, so don't forget to taste some while viewing the gorgeous sunset over the Mediterranean.

EMILY CATLETT

CHAPTER 3

IV. OUTDOOR ACTIVITIES

A. BEACHES AND WATER SPORTS

1. SNORKELING AND DIVING

Snorkeling and diving in Costa Brava is a unique and wonderful experience. The area is home to a rich and diversified marine ecology, with over 500 distinct types of fish, seaweed, and other marine organisms. The warm and tranquil waters of the Mediterranean Sea make it the ideal site for underwater exploration, whether you are a novice or an experienced diver.

One of the primary attractions for snorkelers and divers in Costa Brava is the Medes Islands. This archipelago of seven tiny islands is a recognized marine reserve, and it's regarded to be one of the top diving places in Europe. The crystal blue waters surrounding the islands give a remarkable visibility of up to 50 meters, enabling divers and snorkelers to explore the fascinating underwater world with ease. The Medes Islands are also noted for their amazing underwater rock formations, caverns, and beautiful coral reefs, making them a delight for divers and photographers alike.

For those who like to remain closer to the beach, the tiny and lovely fishing hamlet of Llafranc is a favorite site for snorkeling. Its shallow and tranquil waters are good for novices, and the rocky bottom is filled with colorful schools of fish, making it a fantastic site for underwater photography.

Apart from the Medes Islands and Llafranc, Costa Brava offers several more fantastic sites for snorkeling and diving, including the Aiguafreda Beach, Tamariu, and Calella de Palafrugell. These beaches give easy access to the water, and their rocky shores are home to a variety of marine life, including octopuses, sea urchins, and starfish.

If you are searching for a more demanding diving experience, the wreckage of the Greek cargo ship, the "Marmoler", is an intriguing place to explore. The ship sank in 1974 off the coast of Blanes, and today remains at a depth of 36 meters. The wreck is home to a vast number of fish, including moray eels and groupers, as well as other marine organisms, such as lobsters and crabs.

When it comes to the cost of snorkeling and diving in Costa Brava, it is very reasonable compared to other prominent diving sites. There are several dive shops and facilities that provide equipment rental, guided trips, and diving lessons for all levels. The rates vary depending on the activities you pick, but on average expect to spend roughly €30-€60 for a guided dive or snorkeling experience.

Before going on your snorkeling or diving excursion in Costa Brava, it's vital to bear in mind a few safety recommendations. Always be sure you dive with a companion and never go diving alone.

Familiarize yourself with the local diving laws and obey them rigorously. It's also suggested to undergo a medical check-up before diving and to only dive within your limitations and skills.

2. KAYAKING AND STAND-UP PADDLEBOARDING

Kayaking and SUP are both paddling activities that require utilizing a kayak or a board to travel across the water. While they may look similar, there are several basic distinctions between the two. Kayaking entails using a double-bladed paddle to move a tiny boat, whereas SUP uses a single-bladed paddle to stand on a broader and longer board. Both sports give full-body exercise and an opportunity to immerse oneself in Costa Brava's natural splendor.

One of the greatest ways to enjoy kayaking and SUP in Costa Brava is by joining a guided excursion. These trips frequently start in remote beaches or coves, where you will get a short training on the fundamental skills and safety procedures before setting out. The experts are informed about the region and will take you to the finest areas, where you can delight in the spectacular coastline views and get up close and personal with the rich marine life.

Kayaking and SUP trips in Costa Brava are appropriate for all levels of expertise, so whether you are a novice or a seasoned pro, there is something for everyone. For novices, tranquil and protected waters such as the Aiguablava beach are suitable, while more experienced paddlers may confront the open sea and explore the jagged coastline of Pals Beach.

One of the delights of kayaking and SUP in Costa Brava is the ability to explore secluded coves and caverns that are only accessible by water. As you paddle across the turquoise seas, you will come across spectacular rock formations and majestic cliffs, offering you a unique view of the region's scenery. The guides will also reveal intriguing details about the area's history and look into the local culture.

Apart from the magnificent vistas, kayaking and SUP in Costa Brava also give you the possibility to witness marine life like schools of fish, octopuses, and even dolphins if you are fortunate. The crystal-clear waters give exceptional vision, making it a fantastic pastime for nature lovers and photography aficionados.

The cost of a kayaking or SUP excursion in Costa Brava varies based on the length, location, and inclusions. On average, a half-day trip might cost from €40 to €60 per person, while a full-day excursion can vary from €80 to €100. Some tour operators also provide packages that include transportation, food, and gear rental, making it a hassle-free and value-for-money experience.

3. WINDSURFING AND KITESURFING

1. Costs Involved:

Before going on your windsurfing or kitesurfing trip in Costa Brava, it is crucial to understand the prices involved. The first and most important expenditure would be equipment rental. For windsurfing, you can anticipate spending roughly €30-35 per hour for the rental of board and sail. Kitesurfing equipment rental, on the other hand, may run from €50-60 per hour. If you are a novice, it is advisable to take classes, which may cost roughly €40-50 per hour. Additionally, you may want to consider the cost of transportation to and from the water sports facilities, as well as insurance.

2. Windsurfing at Costa Brava:

Costa Brava is recognized for its constant winds, making it a popular location for windsurfing. One of the greatest sites for windsurfing in Costa Brava is the Bay of Roses. This 4 km long stretch of coastline provides perfect conditions for both beginners and expert windsurfers. Another excellent destination is the hamlet of Sant Pere Pescador, which has shallow seas and consistent breezes, ideal for learning or practicing new skills. The cost of windsurfing in Costa Brava varies from €30-40 per hour for rental and training.

3. Kitesurfing at Costa Brava:

Kitesurfing, commonly known as kiteboarding, is a relatively new but quickly expanding activity in Costa Brava. The Bay of Roses is again a favorite destination for kitesurfing, with its strong and steady winds. However, if you prefer calmer seas, travel to the town of Empuriabrava, renowned as the "Venice of Spain" for its network of canals. This site provides perfect conditions for novices and those wishing to enhance their abilities. The cost of kitesurfing in Costa Brava is somewhat more than windsurfing, with rental and training ranging from €50-60 per hour.

4. Best Time to Visit:

The greatest time to visit Costa Brava for windsurfing and kitesurfing is from May to September when the winds are the highest and the weather is warm. During this period, you can expect average wind speeds of 12-17 knots, suitable for these activities. However, if you want to escape the crowds and enjoy lesser expenses, you may also come in April or October.

5. Tips for a Safe Experience:

While windsurfing and kitesurfing may be thrilling, it is crucial to consider safety. Before setting out, be sure to check the weather and wind conditions. Always wear a life jacket and a wetsuit to protect yourself from the chilly water. It is also important to take training from a licensed teacher to understand the right methods and safety requirements

B. HIKING AND BIKING TRAILS

1. CAMINO DE RONDA

First things first, let's speak about the logistics. The Camino de Ronda is roughly 220 kilometers long, broken into 8 sections, and takes around 10-14 days to complete. You may start the walk from either Blanes or Portbou, and the way is signposted with yellow markers and paint marks. It is crucial to remember that certain portions of the path are rather tough, so it is necessary to be prepared with good footwear and enough of drink. Don't forget to also take some snacks, since you may not come across many restaurants or cafés along the journey.

Now, let's speak about what makes the Camino de Ronda so distinctive. As you stroll, you will be surrounded by spectacular surroundings, from gorgeous coves and crystal blue seas to lush flora and towering cliffs. The path also goes through attractive seaside villages such as Tossa de Mar, Calella de Palafrugell, and Llafranc, where you may stop for a breather and immerse yourself in the local culture. These cities give a terrific chance to enjoy traditional Catalan cuisine, so don't miss out on sampling some excellent paella or fresh seafood.

The Camino de Ronda also has a rich historical and cultural value. This trail was utilized by fishermen and smugglers in the past, and you will come across historic watchtowers and strongholds along the way. These buildings not only contribute to the attractiveness of the walk but also give wonderful vantage spots to take in the views. You will also travel past remote beaches, which can only be accessible by foot, giving a feeling of adventure and exclusivity to your excursion.

As you continue your trip, you will also come across various natural parks, such as Cap de Creus and Aiguamolls de l'Empordà, where you may witness different species and a range of flora and fauna. These parks provide a tranquil setting, excellent for reconnecting with nature.

The Camino de Ronda is not simply a trekking path, but it is also a voyage of self-discovery. As you walk, you will have plenty of time to contemplate, disengage from the rush and bustle of everyday life, and just appreciate the present moment. The rhythm of your walking, the sound of the waves, and the mild sea air will all add to a feeling of serenity and quiet.

2. GR 92 TRAIL

The route starts in the lovely hamlet of Portbou, near the French border, and winds its way past small fishing towns, sandy beaches, and craggy cliffs, before terminating in the popular resort town of Blanes. Along the journey, hikers will be treated to spectacular views of the Mediterranean Sea and will have the chance to find secret coves, explore old ruins, and enjoy the local culture and food.

The GR 92 Trail is appropriate for walkers of all abilities, with several parts presenting differing degrees of difficulty. The well-marked route is highly maintained and widely accessible, making it a popular option for outdoor enthusiasts and wildlife lovers. Embark on this tour and be ready to be astounded by the range of sceneries that the Costa Brava has to offer.

For those wishing to indulge in some leisure and luxury, the GR 92 Trail is surrounded by various magnificent resorts and hotels, where hikers may rest and recharge after a day of hiking. The area is also famed for its traditional Catalan food, so be sure to eat some of the excellent local specialties along the journey.

One of the attractions of the GR 92 Trail is the beautiful Cap de Creus Natural Park. This gorgeous park is home to the easternmost point of Spain and offers hikers a unique environment of rocky cliffs, secluded bays, and panoramic views of the Mediterranean. It's little surprise that this park has been a source of inspiration for artists such as Salvador Dali.

As you make your way down the coast, you will come across numerous wonderful coastal communities, each with its special charm. Cadaqués, with its white-washed homes and meandering alleyways, is a famous place for artists and is also home to the Dali House Museum. The medieval village of Begur features a gorgeous castle and excellent vistas, while Tossa de Mar provides a quaint old town and a stunning beach.

The GR 92 Trail also leads hikers through the Empordà area, famed for its wine production. Make sure to take a pause and try some of the local wines and observe how they are created. With its magnificent scenery, rich history, and wonderful gastronomy, the Costa Brava is an ideal destination for hikers and vacationers alike.

3. GREENWAY ROUTE

The Greenways Route Costa Brava is a network of green trails that run over 125 kilometers, linking the cities of Olot and Girona. Originally constructed along ancient railway lines, the path is today a popular destination for hikers, bikers, and even horse riders.

One of the major charms of the Greenways Route is its stunning scenery, which fluctuates from deep woods to verdant meadows, and from quiet rivers to old volcanic vistas. Along the trip, you will meet magnificent medieval towns, old churches, and gorgeous rural vistas. The varying topography and scenery make the route appropriate for different levels of outdoor activity.

The Route may be separated into three primary portions, each delivering a distinct experience. The first leg, from Olot to Les Planes d'Hostoles, is roughly 30 kilometers and generally level, making it an easy and leisurely walk or bike ride for novices. This segment rewards tourists with wonderful views of Volcanic Park and the majestic Pyrenees.

The second leg, from Les Planes d'Hostoles to Amer, is roughly 47 kilometers and contains some modest inclines, suited for more experienced hikers and bikers. This stretch also provides stunning views of the quaint town of Sant Feliu de Pallerols and its medieval bridge, as well as the Ter River Valley.

The last stage, from Amer to Girona, is roughly 50 kilometers and presents a more demanding terrain. As you reach the finish of your tour, you will travel through gorgeous villages like Santa Pau and La Pera. The tour concludes at the lovely city of Girona, noted for its medieval architecture and lively culture.

Along the road, you will discover many lodging alternatives, ranging from quaint Bed & Breakfasts to expensive hotels. You may also discover several local restaurants providing traditional Catalan food, great for refilling and relishing the tastes of the area.

For those wishing to immerse themselves in nature and unplug from the rush and bustle of daily life, the Greenways Route Costa Brava is the ideal place. The route gives a unique chance to see the beauty of northeastern Spain, its culture, and its people quietly and ecologically.

CHAPTER 4

V. FOOD AND DRINK

A. TRADITIONAL CATALAN CUISINE

1. History and Influences:

Catalonia has a distinct cultural legacy, with its position between the Mediterranean Sea and the Pyrenees Mountains, and its history of being under multiple rulers. This has resulted in a rich culinary culture that is inspired by both land and sea. The region's cuisine is defined by the use of fresh, locally obtained products and uncomplicated cooking methods. Catalan cuisine has also been inspired by nearby areas, like as France, and the Mediterranean nations, resulting in a combination of tastes.

2. Local Ingredients:

The first thing that springs to mind when you think about Catalan cuisine is fish, and for good reason. The Costa Brava's position on the Mediterranean coast means that the area offers an abundance of fresh, high-quality fish. Local fishermen bring in a variety of fish and seafood every day, including sardines, anchovies, mussels, and prawns. These components are utilized in numerous traditional meals, including the renowned grilled sardines, called esqueixada, and spicy seafood stew, known as zarzuela.

Another characteristic of Catalan cuisine is the utilization of seasonal products. The area is endowed with a rich terrain, producing a variety of fruits and vegetables that are utilized in meals such as escalivada, a grilled vegetable dish, and samfaina, a ratatouille-like dish. Locally produced olives and olive oil are also vital components in many meals, lending a powerful and unique taste to the cuisine.

3. Must-Try Dishes:

No journey to the Costa Brava is complete without sampling the classic delicacies that are the glory of Catalan gastronomy. One of the most renowned recipes is pa amb tomàquet, a simple yet wonderful mix of bread, tomato, and olive oil. This dish can be found in practically any restaurant and is great for a fast snack or as a complement to any dinner. Another must-try meal is fideuà, a seafood dish similar to paella but cooked with thin noodles instead of rice. It is a realistic reflection of the region's marine impact.

For meat aficionados, botifarra amb mongetes, a substantial meal of grilled sausage and white beans, is a must-try. And of course, no lunch is complete without a glass of locally made wine. The Costa Brava offers various vineyards that provide tours and tastings, enabling you to enjoy the region's best wines.

4. Sweet Treats:

No vacation is complete without indulging in some traditional sweets, and the Costa Brava offers some wonderful selections. One of the most renowned is crema catalana, a creamy custard dessert with a caramelized sugar topping. Another favorite treat is xuixo, a fried pastry filled with custard or cream. And for chocolate aficionados, try a cup of rich and thick hot chocolate, great for dipping churros or ensaimadas, a sweet pastry akin to a croissant.

B. FAMOUS LOCAL DISHES

1. Paella de Marisco (Seafood Paella)

One cannot speak about Costa Brava food without mentioning Paella de Marisco. This seafood feast is a symphony of tastes, comprising fresh prawns, clams, and mussels, all cooked in saffron-infused rice. Each taste is a celebration of the water, expressing the intimate connection the residents have with their marine environment.

2. Suquet de Peix (Catalan Fish Stew)

Suquet de Peix is a substantial fish stew that represents the spirit of Costa Brava's coastal cuisine. Prepared with the catch of the day and a rich combination of tomatoes, potatoes, and garlic, this stew is both soothing and sumptuous. It's a meal that warms the heart and comforts the spirit, great for a pleasant evening.

3. Escudella i Carn d'Olla

Venture a little inland, and you'll uncover Escudella i Carn d'Olla, a classic Catalan stew. This recipe is a winter classic, mixing meats like chicken, beef, and pig with veggies and rice or pasta. It's a rich, satisfying dinner that brings together families and friends, particularly during celebratory times.

4. Fideuà

Often referred to be the cousin of paella, Fideuà switches out rice for noodles but preserves the flavor of a traditional seafood meal. Cooked in a similar method to paella, it's rich with tastes of the ocean, generally containing a combination of shellfish and fish, all brought together with a hint of garlic and saffron.

5. Crema Catalana

For a sweet conclusion, look to Crema Catalana, Costa Brava's equivalent to crème brûlée. This delectable treat is a creamy custard covered with a coating of firm caramel, frequently seasoned with a dash of cinnamon and lemon zest. It's a simple but exquisite dessert that properly finishes off a dinner.

6. Botifarra amb Mongetes (Sausage with White Beans)

This meal is a rustic and strong blend of grilled pork sausage paired with delicate white beans. The sausage is seasoned with spices peculiar to the area, creating a flavor that is both familiar and strange. It's a meal that exemplifies the simplicity and richness of Catalan cuisine.

7. Anchovies from L'Escala

Last but not least, the anchovies from L'Escala, a little village in Costa Brava, are a must-try. These aren't your typical anchovies. They are delicately filleted, salt-cured, and kept in olive oil, resulting in a delicacy that is both salty and silky.

C. WINE TASTING AND VINEYARD TOURS

1. The Essence of Costa Brava's Wines:

Each bottle of wine from Costa Brava tells a narrative of the peculiar climate and soil that give these wines their special flavor. The region's winemakers are devoted artists who mix old methods with new approaches to produce great wines. From strong reds to crisp whites, Costa Brava's wines are a sensory joy, reflecting the spirit of the Mediterranean.

2. Discovering the Vineyards:

Exploring Costa Brava's wineries is like going into a universe where time slows down, and nature takes center stage. The vineyards, sometimes family-run, provide guided tours where tourists may learn about the wine-making process from grape cultivation to bottling. Walking through rows of grapes, with the background of

Costa Brava's undulating hills and the distant sea, is an experience in itself.

3. Wine Tasting Experiences:

Wine tasting in Costa Brava is not only about drinking and enjoying; it's about connecting with the region and its people. Each tasting session is an educational trip, where sommeliers impart their expertise on the tastes, aromas, and textures of each wine. Visitors get to try a selection of wines, knowing the subtleties that make each one distinctive.

4. Pairing Wine with Local Cuisine:

What better way to appreciate Costa Brava's wines than by mixing them with local delicacies? Many vineyards provide gourmet experiences where wines are combined with regional foods, showcasing the compatibility between local food and wine. From fresh seafood to gourmet cheeses, these combinations are a feast for the senses.

5. Beyond the Vineyard:

Costa Brava's wine culture goes beyond the vineyards. Local towns and markets give an insight into the region's wine tradition, with wine stores and pubs presenting choices from local vineyards. Festivals and wine events throughout the year honor the region's vineyards, adding another layer of pleasure for wine enthusiasts.

CHAPTER 5

VI. NIGHTLIFE AND ENTERTAINMENT

A. BARS AND CLUBS

1. Lloret de Mar: The Heartbeat of Costa Brava's Nightlife

In Lloret de Mar, the night is constantly young, and the energy is electrifying. As the sun falls below the horizon, the streets come alive with a symphony of lights and music. One of the must-visit attractions here is the famed Tropics Disco. With its state-of-the-art sound system and famous DJs spinning the decks, Tropics is a shrine for dance aficionados. Another treasure is Magic Park, featuring a combination of arcade games, karaoke, and dance floors, ideal for a fun-filled night.

2. Blanes: Where Tranquility Meets Fun

Blanes, famed for its stunning beaches and floral gardens, also boasts a more laid-back nightlife. The town's beach bars, or "chiringuitos," provide a comfortable area to sip a beverage with the relaxing sound of waves in the background. For those wanting a colorful setting, Sala Vega is a famous club where locals and visitors alike go to dance the night away.

3. Cadaqués: A Charming Retreat

Cadaqués, with its whitewashed buildings and cobblestone streets, provides a distinct nightlife experience. It's the ideal venue for individuals who want a relaxing evening. Enjoy a drink of local wine at one of the beachside terraces, such as Meliton Bar, which has a spectacular view of the Mediterranean. For a more energetic night, go to Brown Sugar, a club noted for its soulful music and small environment.

4. Platja d'Aro: A Mix of Styles

Platja d'Aro is a flexible venue providing a range of nightlife activities. From stylish beach clubs like Nikki Beach, where you can enjoy a refined cocktail party, to exciting places like Park d'Aro, giving an active environment for party-goers, there's something for everyone.

5. Girona: The Historic Heart's Nighttime Glow

Girona, however more famed for its historical appeal, nevertheless boasts a dynamic night scene. The city's restaurants and pubs, including Sunset Jazz Club, offer an ideal setting for enjoying live music with a glass of good Spanish wine. The old town, with its evocative streets, is home to several secret taverns where you may experience local life.

Tips for a Perfect Night Out in Costa Brava

1. Dress Code: Most clubs have a casual-chic dress code, so dress appropriately.

2. Timing: Remember, the night begins late in Spain. Many clubs don't begin rolling till late.

3. Safety: While Costa Brava is typically safe, please be aware of your things.

4. Native Delicacies: Don't miss out on enjoying native beverages, including Cava or Sangria.

B. LIVE MUSIC VENUES

1. Calella de Palafrugell – The Jardí Botànic de Cap Roig

Imagine a botanical garden turned into a theater beneath the stars. The Cap Roig Festival, held yearly in Calella de Palafrugell, provides precisely that. This unusual location, with its amphitheater ringed by beautiful flora and overlooking the Mediterranean Sea, showcases a diversity of worldwide acts. From pop to classical, each event here is a celebration of nature and music.

2. Girona – Sunset Jazz Club

Girona, a city where history breathes through its old walls, is home to the Sunset Jazz Club. This compact venue, with its comfortable environment, is great for people who like the seductive and deep sounds of jazz. It's a location where artists and audience members feel a deep connection, sharing a passion for improvised melodies and rhythmic blues.

3. Lloret de Mar - The Gardens of Santa Clotilde

Lloret de Mar is not only about bustling nightlife; it's also home to the peaceful Gardens of Santa Clotilde. These ancient gardens provide a lovely environment for live music concerts, especially during the summer months. As you listen to live performances, surrounded by the beautiful scenery and the aroma of blossoming flowers, the experience is both captivating and refreshing.

4. Palafrugell – Havaneres Festival

Palafrugell's Havaneres Festival is a cultural fixture, honoring traditional Catalan sea shanties known as 'Havaneres'. This event, situated along the shore, offers a nostalgic but energetic environment. Singers and ensembles present these emotional tunes that relate stories of the sea, love, and desire, letting the listener connect with Costa Brava's naval tradition.

5. Tossa de Mar - The Ancient Walls

In Tossa de Mar, music echoes behind old walls. This ancient town, with its medieval splendor, periodically converts its old town into a live music venue. Walking through the stone streets, one may come across many styles of music, from local folk melodies to modern hits, all reverberating off the old walls, providing a weird and timeless experience.

6. Figueres – Teatre-Museu Dalí

Although largely recognized for its association with Salvador Dalí, the Teatre-Museu Dalí in Figueres also organizes distinctive musical concerts. The merging of Dalí's surrealistic paintings with live music gives an unparalleled sensory experience. Whether it's a classical concert or a current music performance, the venue ensures a fantastic evening.

7. Roses - Sons del Món Festival

Roses, with its magnificent beaches and crystal-clear seas, is also the venue of the Sons del Món Festival. This event brings together wine, food, and music. Imagine drinking on great local wine while listening to live music, with the background of the Mediterranean Sea — it's a feast for all the senses.

C. FESTIVALS AND EVENTS

1. Festival de la Luz (Festival of Light) - December

As the year winds down, San José, the capital city, lights up with the Festival de la Luz, a beautiful spectacle that marks the beginning of the Christmas season. Imagine a night parade where floats decked with thousands of lights glide through the streets, accompanied by exciting music and dancing performances. It's a magnificent event that brings together families and friends, connecting them in a festival of light and love.

2. Fiestas Palmares - January

Kick out the new year with Fiestas Palmares, a two-week spectacle celebrated in the little town of Palmares. This event is a real expression of Costa Rican culture, offering everything from bullfights and horse parades to live bands and local delicacies. It's a time when the town changes into a busy carnival, giving unlimited entertainment and pleasure for all ages.

3. Envision Festival - February

For anyone seeking a combination of spirituality, art, music, and nature, the Envision Festival is a must-visit. Set in the picturesque seaside hamlet of Uvita, this festival is a celebration of sustainable living and creativity. Attend yoga classes, dance to the rhythms of foreign music, engage in creative workshops, and interact with like-minded folks in an eco-friendly setting. It's more than simply a festival; it's a movement towards a more aware and connected society.

4. Semana Santa (Holy Week) - March/April

Semana Santa, or Holy Week, is a strongly religious and culturally important period in Costa Rica. It's a week of somber processions, reenactments of the Passion of Christ, and contemplative thought. This time shows the rich Catholic tradition of the nation, with each town contributing its particular twist to the observances. It's a time for families to gather together and partake in age-old rituals.

5. Carnaval de Limón - October

Experience the Afro-Caribbean influence on Costa Rican culture during the Carnaval de Limón. This boisterous event in the harbor city of Limón is highlighted by colorful costumes, calypso music, and enthusiastic parades. It's a celebration of variety and tradition, where the rhythms of the Caribbean combine effortlessly with Costa Rican flare, creating an environment of contagious energy and delight.

6. Fiesta de los Diablitos - December/January

The Fiesta de los Diablitos, or 'Festival of the Little Devils,' is a unique traditional event observed by the Boruca people. This ceremony commemorates the fight of the indigenous people against

Spanish occupation, with villagers wearing devil masks and participating in pretend combat. It's a strong display of cultural identity and perseverance, looking for the rich fabric of Costa Rica's indigenous past.

7. Coffee Harvest Festival - November

Costa Rica's world-renowned coffee is honored each year during the Coffee Harvest Festival. Held in coffee-rich districts like Naranjo and San Marcos, this event pays respect to the country's coffee-growing legacy. Enjoy a cup of the best Costa Rican coffee, learn about the coffee-making process, and engage in the vibrant festivities that feature music, dancing, and, of course, lots of coffee tasting.

CHAPTER 6

VII. PRACTICAL INFORMATION

A. TRANSPORTATION OPTIONS

1. Car Rental

Renting a vehicle is by far the most convenient and flexible method to see Costa Brava. The area boasts a well-maintained network of roads, making it simple to traverse and visit all of its renowned locations. There are multiple automobile rental firms present at the airports and main cities, providing different car types at cheap prices. The anticipated cost for a week-long automobile rental varies from €150-€300, depending on the car type and rental time.

2. Train

The train is another quick and pleasant method to move around Costa Brava. The area has two important railway lines, RENFE and FGC, linking its towns and cities. RENFE serves the seaside towns while FGC links the interior towns. The trains operate often, and the costs are inexpensive, with one-way tickets beginning at €5. However, it is worth noting that the rail network does not serve all sites in Costa Brava, so it may not be a great alternative for people wishing to explore off-the-beaten-path spots.

3. Bus

Costa Brava boasts a dependable and large network of buses that link its numerous villages and cities. The largest bus operator in the area is Sarfa, operating both local and long-distance trips. Bus tickets are usually cheaper than rail tickets, with costs beginning at €1.50 for short rides. However, going by bus might take longer, and schedules may not always be dependable, so it is vital to prepare properly.

4. Taxi

Taxis are frequently accessible in Costa Brava, especially in famous tourist destinations. They are a great solution for shorter flights or individuals traveling with large baggage. Taxis in the area operate on a meter system, so be careful to check the fee with the driver before starting your trip. A typical taxi journey in Costa Brava might cost anything from €10-€20.

5. Bicycle

For the more daring and eco-conscious guests, renting a bicycle is a wonderful way to discover Costa Brava. The area boasts a well-developed network of bike lanes, making it safe and pleasurable to appreciate its natural beauty on two wheels. There are various bike rental businesses available, with costs ranging from €10-€20 per day.

6. Walking

Last but not least, walking is an outstanding method to appreciate the beauty of Costa Brava. Many of its towns and villages are tiny and pedestrian-friendly, making it simple to explore on foot. Moreover, walking enables you to uncover hidden jewels and absorb them in the local environment at your speed, all while saving on transit expenditures.

B. SAFETY AND EMERGENCY NUMBERS

When going to a foreign nation, it is strongly important to be acquainted with the local emergency numbers. In Costa Brava, the emergency number is 112. It is a toll-free number that may be called on any phone, including landlines and mobile phones. 112 links you to the emergency services, including police, fire brigade, and ambulance.

In case of any emergency, do not hesitate to phone 112. It is a 24/7 service, and the operators are bilingual, making it simpler for travelers to convey their difficulties.

Besides the main emergency number, particular numbers might be more advantageous in different circumstances. If you want medical treatment, you may contact 061. It is the national medical emergency service in Spain, and they will transport an ambulance to your area quickly.

In case of a fire emergency, phone 085 to contact the local fire department. It is governed by the regional government and is responsible for managing fire-related situations. In Costa Brava, there are additional emergency services specializing in rescuing individuals from mountains or water, which can be accessed by phoning 080.

Apart from emergency numbers, it is usually a good idea to have the contact information of your country's embassy in Costa Brava. In case you lose your passport, experience legal challenges, or need any other help, the embassy may give the required support and counsel.

Precaution is crucial when it comes to keeping safe when traveling. Before departing on your Costa Brava adventure, be sure to investigate and be informed of any possible risks, including harsh weather conditions or natural catastrophes. It is also important to get travel insurance that covers medical emergencies and repatriation.

Another crucial component of keeping safe is to be aware of your surroundings. Avoid going alone at night, particularly in unknown locations. It is also advisable to keep your important possessions near to you and avoid exhibiting them in public.

When visiting the beaches in Costa Brava, always pay attention to the caution flags. Red flags signify high-danger circumstances, and it is suggested to avoid swimming in the water. Yellow flags suggest caution, while green flags imply it is okay to swim.

In case of any suspicious or illegal activity, do not hesitate to notify the police at 091. The police are regarded to be competent and friendly to visitors, however, it is always advisable to avoid any unsafe circumstances.

C. TIPS FOR TRAVELING WITH CHILDREN

1. Plan and Be Flexible

One of the main components of a successful family vacation is preparing beforehand. Make careful to explore the location and plan out your agenda ahead of time. This will help you prevent any last-minute stress and guarantee that you enjoy a well-rounded experience. However, it's also crucial to be flexible and accept that with small children, things don't always go as planned. Be prepared to make modifications and adjustments as required to prevent any outbursts or meltdowns.

2. Choose the Right Accommodations

When traveling with children, it's crucial to find the correct lodgings that will accommodate your family's requirements. Look for hotels or vacation rentals with facilities like a pool, playground, or kids' club. This will make your stay more pleasurable for both you and your tiny ones. Additionally, consider a location that is convenient to the major attractions and has good access to public transit, so you don't have to trek great distances with weary children.

3. Pack Smart

Packing for a family vacation may be intimidating, but with a little forethought, it can be a snap. Make a list of all the things your children will need, such as diapers, food, and games to keep them engaged during lengthy flights or car drives. It's also a good idea to bring some medication for any unforeseen illnesses or injuries. Don't forget to bring sunscreen and caps to protect your youngsters from the sun's rays.

4. Enjoy the Beach Life

Costa Brava is famed for its magnificent beaches, and what's more enjoyable for youngsters than playing on the sand and splashing in the waves? Make sure you include beach toys and floaties for your small ones to enjoy. There are also lots of seaside restaurants and cafés where you can get a bite to eat, making it simple to spend the full day at the beach with your family.

5. Explore the Outdoors

Costa Brava is a haven for environment enthusiasts, and youngsters will undoubtedly be impressed by the lush woods, towering cliffs, and crystal-clear seas. Take your family on a picturesque trek along the seaside pathways or hire bicycles to explore the region together.

You may also embark on a boat excursion to find secret coves and caves along the coast, which will be a unique experience for youngsters.

6. Engage in Local Cuisine

Don't forget to indulge in the great local food throughout your stay in Costa Brava. While it's tempting to stick to meals that are familiar to your children, encourage them to try new things. From fresh seafood to Mediterranean tapas, there's something for everyone to enjoy. You may also visit local markets to pick up fresh fruits and snacks for your small ones.

7. Stay Safe

It's crucial to consider safety, particularly when traveling with children. Make sure to keep a tight check on them at all times and educate them about safety regulations, such as remaining near to you in busy locations and avoiding chatting with strangers. Also, develop a strategy in case somebody gets separated, such as a prearranged meeting point.

D. SUSTAINABLE TOURISM INITIATIVES

One of the primary projects for sustainable tourism in Costa Brava is the preservation of its natural environment. The area boasts of gorgeous beaches, crystal clear waterways, and varied flora and wildlife. To conserve these unique resources, the government has developed efforts to mitigate the effect of tourism such as implementing rigorous waste management programs and encouraging eco-friendly transportation alternatives.

Tourists are urged to participate in responsible activities such as snorkeling, hiking, and bird-watching, which not only decrease negative consequences but also increase respect and knowledge of the natural environment.

In terms of cultural sustainability, Costa Brava has made attempts to maintain its rich legacy and customs. The area is home to various attractive towns and villages where tourists may experience the true Catalan way of life. To minimize the detrimental impacts of mass tourism on the local culture, measures such as cultural education programs and engagement of the local population in tourist activities are being developed. This not only helps to safeguard cultural identity but also produces a more meaningful and genuine experience for tourists.

Sustainable tourism also entails economic sustainability, and Costa Brava has taken measures to ensure that the local economy benefits from visitors. Small and locally-owned companies are promoted, and visitors are urged to purchase local items and support the community. This not only helps to divide the economic advantages of tourism among the local community but also encourages a more sustainable and responsible travel experience.

Another key part of sustainable tourism in Costa Brava is the encouragement of responsible and courteous conduct among guests. Visitors are instructed on the dos and don'ts of responsible tourism, such as respecting local customs and traditions, preserving resources, and reducing trash. This provides a more beneficial influence on the environment and local people and also encourages tourists to follow similar sustainable habits in their journeys.

Furthermore, Costa Brava has also made initiatives to limit its carbon footprint and minimize its influence on the environment. Eco-friendly lodgings, such as hotels and campsites, are marketed and visitors are urged to utilize public transit or select for eco-tourism activities that have a smaller environmental effect. The usage of renewable energy sources is also being encouraged, with projects such as solar-powered boats and electric buses gaining favor.

EMILY CATLETT

CONCLUSION

In the pages of our Costa Brava Travel Guide 2024, we have gone on an incredible adventure through one of the most charming and scenic locations in the world. We've unearthed hidden treasures, toured lively cities, and enjoyed the engaging culture of Costa Brava. As we close our guide, let's take a minute to summarize the vital information we've acquired during our voyage, and I hope you'll feel motivated to make Costa Brava your next vacation destination.

1. Breathtaking Beaches: We've dived into the beautiful beaches of Costa Brava, from the quiet coves of Cadaqués to the crowded shoreline of Lloret de Mar. Whether you desire seclusion or mingling, Costa Brava offers a beach for you.

2. Cultural Riches: The region's rich past is evident in its architecture, museums, and festivals. Don't miss the opportunity to discover the historic alleyways of Girona or immerse yourself in the bizarre world of Salvador Dalí in Figueres.

3. Culinary Delights: Costa Brava is a gourmet wonderland. From fresh seafood to Catalan favorites like paella and crema catalana, every meal is an extraordinary experience.

4. Outdoor Adventures: Nature aficionados will find their paradise at Costa Brava. Hiking in the Cap de Creus Natural Park, kayaking

along the craggy coastline, or cycling through vineyards - the alternatives are unlimited.

5. Charming towns: Discover scenic towns like Tossa de Mar, Begur, and Pals, where time seems to stand still, and the spirit of Costa Brava's beauty comes to life.

6. Local Insights: Throughout this book, we've advised locals, guaranteeing that you'll see Costa Brava like a seasoned visitor.

As we conclude off our voyage around the wonderful Costa Brava, I invite you to take that leap of faith, to book your ticket, pack your luggage, and start on your adventure. The beauty, culture, and kindness of this area await your exploration. Whether you're a sun-seeker, a history buff, a gourmet, or an adventurer, Costa Brava has something to offer every tourist.

So, my reader, I dare you to let the charm of Costa Brava weave its spell on you. Choose to discover this beautiful place in 2024 and make experiences that will last a lifetime. The gorgeous beaches, the rich culture, the scrumptious food, and the warm natives are waiting to welcome you with open arms. Don't miss out on the trip of a lifetime Costa Brava awaits, and your journey starts today.

Printed in Great Britain
by Amazon

44382544R00056